CORE LEADERSHIP SERIES VOLUME 1

PARADIGM SHIFT

SECOND ADDITION

BUILDING A FOUNDATION OF CHURCH LEADERSHIP FROM THE INSIDE OUT

Johnny M. Wilson, Jr.

FOREWORD BY

Doris Hooks

ISBN: 978-621-434-052-1 (Softcover)
978-621-434-053-8 (Hardcover)

Printed in New York by:

OMNIBOOK CO.
99 Wall Street, Suite 118
New York, NY 10005
USA
+1 202-738-1322
www.omnibookcompany.com

First Edition

For e-book purchase: Kindle on Amazon, Barnes and Noble
Book purchase: Amazon.com, Barnes & Noble, and www.omnibookcompany.com
Omnibook titles may be purchased in bulk for educational, business, fund-raising, or sales promotional use. For more information please e-mail info@omnibookcompany.com

Cover Design by Gian Carlo Tan

ACKNOWLEDGMENTS

First acknowledgement to the Olney Street Baptist Church and the members that have supported my ministry for many years. The faithfulness of those that have blessed me with their tears of joy, sadness and hopes. To the many friends and alumni of American Baptist Seminary of the West at Berkeley and to my home church Allen Temple Baptist Church and the pastoral leadership of Dr. James Alfred Smith Sr. Pastor Emeritus and Dr. James Alfred Smith Jr. Pastor for their support throughout the years.

Special thanks to my advisor of my doctorate program at United Theological Seminary Dr. Robert Walker and Dr. Linda Thomas, PhD. Also, Reverend Dr. Doris Hooks, Pastor of International Community Church in Boston, MA.

To my late father Deacon, Dad, Johnny M. Wilson Sr. that has given me so much of a life for being the clergy person that I am today. Finally, to my Mother Nathalie C. Wilson and my dearly beloved Levonne for the years of ministry.

"Consequently, you are no longer foreigners and strangers, but fellow citizens with God's people and also members of his household, built on the foundation of the apostles and prophets, with Christ Jesus himself as the chief cornerstone."

Ephesians 2:19-20 NIV

CONTENTS

FOREWORD

Paradigm Shift gives us a liberating view of struggles and challenges that all clergy face when dealing with congregational memberships who hold on tightly to many traditions that are more reflective of prestige and authority and not biblical teachings. These traditions places more value on self edification than on love of God, or love of others. This book also gives the opportunity for clergy to gather and have a reflective dialog on developing new ideas; new pathways to building a stronger and more enduring church body. A body that stays in place and not scatter.

As a Pastor, who just so happens to be female, we are faced with many obstacles that have become impediments to successful leadership. When it comes to defining and executing plans for initiatives leading to change, church membership quickly begin to actively explore ways to halt new ideas of inclusiveness. Moving the church forward to embrace change is the life of the church. The spiritual health and sound biblical education of the membership is the undergirding needed for future growth and survival of the church. Paradigm Shift helps to make stronger visions that propels the congregation to move forward. Most would call this … stepping out on faith.

For a large population of church membership, the idea of change is met with suspicion and intimidation. The underlying idea that church folk believe they will lose their "promised land" by embracing change, renders them defensive, fragmented and filled with fear. This has become the battleground to conquer. I am reminded of David and Goliath from the Old Testament book of 1st Samuel. This Davidic event shows us that for 40 days, no one would face the Philistine weapon, the giant Goliath. For hundreds of years, the Philistines slowly encroached and seized the promise land of the Israelites. The Valley of Elah would seem

to be their final battle ground and the giant challenged the Israel's a
twice each day with shouts of confrontation. The Israelites were losi
Finally, after 40 days of hearing Goliath shouting out his challenge,
Israelite army was delivered by a teenage boy with a rock and a sli
David finally accepted the challenge of Goliath The giant was kill
with one blow from the rock thrown by David because God was wi
him. The faith of David was absolute. He steps out on foundation
faith in God along with quite a bit of "chutzpah" I may add! The gian
was slain, the land and it's inhabitants were saved. If we want to sav
our promised land (our beloved church) and if we want to deliver ou
people, clergy must demonstrate to God that we have that kind of faith.
Faith that will allow us to step out and stand in strength and purpose; and not fall. It is a challenge to all who desires to answer the call of discipleship. Rev. Dr. Wilson tells us in this book, … there is ministry in challenges. King David ushered in a new era because he accepted the challenge, trusted in the Lord and let Him fight his battle. The church is challenged to move toward change and the church body will not trust God to fight it.

I find that this book lends itself to be a much needed asset for shaping the battle strategy of church growth for such a time as this. The possibilities are bountiful and we must know that all obstacles can be conquered if we only believe and place trust in God and embrace servant leadership. When it is of God, it will not fail. Paradigm Shift delivers a learned discipline of leadership and values that can assist with moving the church forward in developing new ways to embrace new relationships. It is showing the church how to become involved with communities; to take a journey and work together to discover a bold new dynamic face of discipleship in Jesus Christ. After all, isn't that what we are charged to do?

Congratulations to Rev. Dr. Wilson! You have given us a model pathway of building a new community; one that is established in love with Christ at the helm!

Rev. Dr. Doris Barron-Hooks

INTRODUCTION

The book describes some of the challenges facing clergy, lay folks, and organization structure as it relates to governance in local church, social change and the power of congregation conflict plays in the life of the local church. As I started in my first book, that I felt that "Churches that are traditional in all aspects of church life are sometimes fearful of spiritual renewal and servant leadership. This servant leadership model trained clergy with a vision toward spiritual and development are sometimes and educational ideas that change the constitutions of the church toward improvements and growth".

In the first edition I stated that change is problematic within congregations.

Many social service agencies such as: the red cross, neighborhood centers in combination with non-profits provide a special social service to many families needing food to survive and basic living essentials. An article by the Center on Budget and Policy Priorities dated March 18, 2016 by Ed Bolen, Dottie Rosenbaum, Stacy Dean, and Brynner Keith-Jennings asserts that more *than 500,000 and as many as 1 million of the nation's poorest people will be cut off snap over the course of 2016.*

The history of the past defines traditional model of leadership; customs, culture, special days for specific groups and social ministry that are more internal than outreach.

Finally, trust is the key to bringing about lasting working relationships with local conservative congregations. The book is divided into four chapters. Chapter 1 is "Tradition and Change", chapter two is "Tradition from the Inside Out" and chapter 3 is "Core Foundations". The final chapter some personal thoughts with conclusion. There are several vital resources that contributed to excellent resources as it relates to change in thinking to organizational development. I have noted in the book, ***Heart and Head, Dr. Dwight Hopkins*** provides an accurate study on the impact social transformation of wicked structures and destructive system. The author insights on some causes of social plight against humanity of which the "least of the community is at the mercy of society. Many of these churches in poor communities lack the leadership development for reaching within the community. Many of the people in the community need mental health counseling and conflict resolution with displaced families. A review of the model of ministry for learning opportunities is describes as a suitable model for inclusive community, building ideals for faith communities such as churches, non-profits, and educational institutions.

The chapter on ***Core Foundations*** provides examples of how change can meet the need for those seeking grounding to what it means for have some connection to core values as it relates to theological understanding on "equipping folks for more "earthly work. **Author Edgar H. Schein, in his work organizational Culture**, introduces a model of change comprised of five specific steps: (1). Specifying goals, (2). Comparing the present status with the first ideal. (3). Dealing with tension, (4). Developing a plan for change and (5). Revisiting goals and the vision is not resolved in a productive way.

Change is challenging for it beings about new opportunities to struggle with those issues that are often uncomfortable to appreciate. The book describes the challenges of the stronghold of churches that are rich in developing and envision their own purpose. The group is well-organized from within the local church of which many have held position for more than forty years in the Church. pastor facing resistance throughout the author's ministry despite educational development that is part of the old conservative way of operating in the local church.

In September 2004, this author completed a three-day retreat at Allen Temple Baptist Church in Oakland, California. The men's retreat has been a Men's Ministry for more than twentyfive years. Topics ranged from men's health, relationships, and fellowship. After spending time at Redwood Forest in North California and returning to New England, this author returned home and asked the following question. "How can renewal begin within the church, ***from the inside out?***"

A little voice responded, ***"Reverend, you have to be patient."***

Change is a complex problem at any church and for any congregation. Traditional churches are facing change and challenges never experienced before it is imperative that congregations continue to change, meaning to become friendlier and get involved more in the lives of the congregation. ***Change is a time of risk, resistance, and conflict,*** issues that this author will address from a congregational model on ***building relationships in the faith community.***

This book is the result of years of observation into the lives of parishioners attending to the religious experiences of people struggling, making a difference and a surviving legacy in a changing world. ***Building a community of faith among church members and leaders is essential to future generations.*** It is the ***leader's challenge*** to learn from past successes and failures to advance positive change by fostering relationships in every aspect of ministry and support.

TRADITION AND CHANGE

CHAPTER ONE

One of the most complicated parts of church life is working in a diversified community where differences of opinions, lack of communication, and unwanted change create tension. The lack of meaningful dialogue creates unfair treatment of church constituents. The lack of trust without some healthy form of communication creates suspicion on how churches and congregation carry out their daily operations and affairs.

In this ***global society***, change is a never ending ***struggle*** which is eternally a work in process. Similarly, change within the church provides an opportunity to explore different areas of interest and provide for dialogue and new ways of building relationships and reducing the distrust that comes with working in the local church and ministry.

In my upbringing in the 1960s and 1970s, both my parents developed my talent and skill with an open ***heart*** to believe in myself during a time of ***racism, segregation, and bigotry.*** Through continual ***struggles and challenges***, I learned the value of ***love, dignity, and the appreciation of human life.*** The attributes of ***struggle, love and dignity***

created the opportunity to build positive relationships and served as a ***catalyst*** against the injustices in society. Additionally, it empowered me to develop leadership skills toward supporting families in need that were experiencing spiritual distress.

My college education at the Southern University at Baton Rouge was inexpertly interrupted, by a student demonstration because of the Vietnam War. Leonard D. Brown and Denver Smith was killed at the university in November 1972. Thus, the campus was closed for one semester to "regroup" from the unrest until the fall of 1973. At that time, I transferred to the University of Louisiana, Monroe (formally the Northeast Louisiana University of Monroe).

Throughout my second year of college, I focused on working for change: to grant equal and civil rights to all students on campus. In the early 1970s, black pride became synonymous with the need for positive change for African American Students.

During the spring semester of 1974, the student government invited me to introduce the speaker for an annual student government event, the late Reverend Ralph Abernathy. In 1975, Reverend Abernathy was the President of the Southern Christian Leadership Conference. This experience has pushed me even further to develop positive relationships and facilitate change for those who needed it in their lives.

The experiences of injustice were truly a way of life. The circumstances of emotional desire to improve one's status were always complicated by the voices and forces of injustice. For me, the spirit of Christ and centered my thoughts around the positive energy of a shift of good and grace. The idea of hope for one's living in this world requires a shift to a new focus and a new beginning from the pain of life. We must learn to shift away from that which is destructive and hopeless of which I call, a Paradigm Shift.

Different church groups have special celebrative days, such as Children's Day, Women's Day, and Men's Day. The church also celebrates its anniversary once each year and has special services that correlate with its special days.

The church covenant is basic to the mission of the church. It is a verbal contract, built on traditional African American Baptist principles and reads as follows:

Having been ***led***, as we believe, by the ***Spirit of God*** to receive ***the Lord Jesus Christ as our savior***; and on the profession of our faith, having been baptized in the ***name of the Father, and of the Son, and of the Holy Spirit,*** we do now in the ***presence of God, angels, and this assembly,*** most solemnly and joyfully enter covenant with one another, as one body in Christ. We engage, therefore, by the aid of the ***Holy Spirit,*** to walk together in ***Christian love***; to strive for the advancement of this church in ***knowledge and holiness***; to give it a place in our affections, prayers, and services above every organization of human origin; to sustain its worship, ordinances, discipline, and doctrine; to contribute cheerfully and regularly, as ***God has prospered us,*** toward its expenses, for the support of a faithful and evangelical ministry among us, ***the relief of the poor, and the spread of the Gospel throughout the world.*** In case of differences of opinion in the church, we will strive to avoid a contentious spirit and if we cannot unanimously agree, we will cheerfully recognize the right of the majority to govern. We also engage to maintain family and secret devotion; to ***study diligently the word of God;*** to religiously educate our children; to seek the salvation of our kindred and acquaintance; to walk circumspectly in the world; to be ***kind and just*** to those in our employ, and faithful in the service we promise others; endeavoring in the ***purity of heart*** and ***good will toward all men*** to exemplify and commend our holy faith. We further engage to watch over, to pray for, to exhort and stir up each other unto every good deed and work; to guard each other's reputation, not needlessly exposing the infirmities of others; to participate in each other's joy and with tender sympathy bear one another's burdens and sorrows;

to cultivate ***Christian courtesy;*** to be slow to give or take offense, but always ready for reconciliation, being mindful of the ***rules of the Savior*** in the eighteenth chapter of Matthew, to secure it without delay; and through life, amid He called us out of darkness into His marvelous light. When we're removed from this place, we engage as soon as possible to unite with some other church where we can carry out the spirit of this covenant and the principles of God's Word.

The church covenant is one voice within some Baptist Churches. It speaks of a traditional of faithful folks that worked in the cotton fields of the south and in the factories in the north and deal with the injustices of food, housing and shelter. This covenant speaks to a focus on God in the face of hurt and pain and knowing that God is their strength in the time of trouble and in good times.

The heart of the spiritual community of any Christian Church is the solidarity among people of faith. The bonds between members are not formal or structured but are ***freeflowing and other expressions of agape love.*** The real flesh and blood manifestations of ecclesia, however, are found in the tension with the institutional tendencies inherent within all churches. As Emil Brunner puts it:

> ***THE BROTHERHOOD CAN HAVE LAWS AND INSTITUTIONS, BUT IT CAN NEVER REGARD THESE AS BELONGING TO ITS ESSENCE. BUT, ABOVE ALL, IT CAN NEVER UNDERSTAND ITSELF AS AN INSTITUTION… AND THIS NON-INSTITUTIONAL CHARACTER IS MUCH MORE EVIDENT STILL IN THE ECCLESIA OF THE NEW TESTAMENT WHOSE LIFE-ELEMENT IS THE HOLY SPIRIT".***

Many churches teach and derive its basic theological purpose from the King James Version of the Bible. The word of God is proclaimed, and the petitions of the people are offered in worship. The Bible is the

authoritative document for basic instruction and for spiritual enrichment and insight. Despite any internal struggles all churches have, its ***people are encouraged*** by the preached word and the celebration of how God has provided purpose and direction for the congregation.

The church also exists to call on people to experience ***newness of life in Christ.***

TRADITION FROM INSIDE OUT

CHAPTER TWO

The operative beliefs in many congregations are based on the ***power of the written word.*** Church members possess a definite ***belief in God*** and an obligation to articulate, interpret and access the doctrinal affirmations of the church. They also realize they have a responsibility for caring for the community of faith. For many churches (African American) preaching is the focus on Sunday worship. Preaching is a transformative process that speaks to the pain, joy and hope on what the gospel of Jesus Christ, can and will do, for the faithful. The objective is the idea that the children of God, must conform or be committed to the unconditional surrender in the local church. The conservative objective challenges the preacher to lead people to dedicate themselves and all the resources under God. The preaching event can be a story, devotional or sometimes doctrinal. One of the most important aspects to the preaching setting is the supportive objective. A pastoral style reaches into the soul of those that have suffered and are sufferings with the spirit of the living of these days. Prophetic preaching comes out of the heart of the "people", with the thrust of hope for a better day in the lives of the least of the community of faith. The biblical teachings provide ***a hopeful response*** to the present-day concerns of society.

The church had several auxiliaries that operate as separate, but connected, entities. The Deacon Board, for example, had the freedom to act and develop their own programs and policies. These boards planned the traditional activities of the church each year and the finances of the church, which were overseen by the Board of Trustees. The deacons were responsible for visiting the sick, serving communion, and providing special support to the widows of the congregation.

Celebrative African American worship is in great demand at churches. The joy of worship is ***an ecstatic expression of reverence to God.*** It is the empowering and redemptive work of hope in the congregation. The music, the prayers and the delivery of sermons are the main elements that drive the survival of folks that are hungry for spiritual guidance and nurturing in many churches. ***Like Moses, Miriam and the Israelites, African American folks celebrate their suffering, pain, racism, and injustice as something God has brought them through.***

This author's philosophy of pastoral leadership is to teach others the importance of ***taking responsibility*** for different ministry aspects of the church, including administration, finance, new membership development, evangelism, missions, and stewardship. This author believes that ***building strong relationships among lay folks in the congregation is essential on promoting the overall health of the congregation.*** The lack of positive communication and relationships, limits the church's ability to be effective in all areas of ministry. Positive communication and relationship building is key in a pastor's leadership style of being effective as well.

Relationships are vital to any organization and to the development of church members. People are dependent upon relationships that bring ***change and hopeful outcomes.*** If any congregation and group of lay leadership is to continue the work of the Kingdom of God, it must experience ***freedom*** in the local church. Freedom to change and impact a more positive nature of interaction.

The account of raising Lazarus from the dead is a biblical example of life and transformation. ***John 11:38-44 reminds us:***

> *Then Jesus, again greatly disturbed, came to the tomb. It was a cave, and a stone was lying against it. Jesus said, "Take away the stone." Martha, the sister of the dead man, said to him, "Lord, already there is a stench because he has been dead four days." Jesus said to her, "Did I not tell you that if you believed, you would see the glory of God? "Therefore, they took away the stone. In addition, Jesus looked upward and said, "Father, I thank you for having heard me. I knew that you always hear me, but I have said this for the sake of the crowd standing here, so that they may believe that you sent me." When he had said this, he cried with a loud voice, "Lazarus, come out!" The dead man came out, his hands and feet bound with strips of cloth, and his face wrapped in a cloth. Jesus said to them, "Unbind him, and let him go" (Jn. 11:38-44 NRSV).*

The heart of the church is its connectedness to people discovering each other's ***strengths*** and leading each other in dialogue. Without the commitment of building meaningful relationships, (change in thinking) communication will cease and the ministry of the Kingdom of God would have been limited. Even with the best intentions of worship and prayer, if leaders lack the spiritual fabric to interact with folks, the local church will limit its effectiveness toward change and social transformation.

In second Cor. 5:16-19 NKJV, Paul addresses the church on the importance of newness in Christ:

> *Where henceforth know we no man after the flesh; yea though we have known Christ after the flesh, yet now henceforth know us him no more. Therefore, if any man is in Christ, he is a new creature; old things are passed away; behold, all things are become new. In addition, all things are of God, who hath reconciled us to himself by Jesus Christ, and hath given to us the ministry of reconciliation; to wit, that God was in Christ, reconciling the world unto him, not imputing their trespasses unto them; and hath committed unto us the word of reconciliation (2 Cor. 5:16-19 NKJV).*

How can leaders of the church be motivated to become involved in the community? Is the ministry of reconciliation a challenge? Is change possible for traditional congregations?

Reflecting on the Prophet Ezekiel, a spiritual and social concern is present. In Judah's society, ***the lack of motivation and the appreciation of the power of the all-wise and mighty Creator contributed to the nation's fall into Babylonian control. The inability to adapt and navigate the needs of the oppressed became the legacy of this nation. Eze. 11:19NASB envisioned for the people "a new spirit within them."***

If the local church is to survive and move forward in the future as it has in the past, it must achieve solid working relationships to be able to work together to achieve a common vision.

In Matthew, chapter 4, upon hearing the hopeful words of Jesus, ***"Follow me, and I will make you fishermen of people,"*** the disciples "immediately" left their comfort zones of life. The fear of change is the fear of being out of control. As churches and congregations look ahead to a time when they may face different styles of worship, music, and leadership, they will fear no longer having control over their ministries. Fear is not always expressed and the opportunity to share is not always possible among leaders and church members, even though these things are vital to the church.

Edwin H. Friedman's book, Family Process, and Organization Life, stresses the complex dual relationships in the family church, and how the family model plays a large role in a congregational family church. He asserts:

> *A FAMILY BUSINESS, FOR EXAMPLE, WILL MIRROR IN ITS OWN SYSTEM THE EMOTIONAL PROCESSES GOING ON IN THE FAMILY THAT RUNS IT. (THIS IS ALSO TRUE OF SMALLTOWN CHURCHES.) INDEED, IT IS ALMOST IMPOSSIBLE TO BRING CHANGE TO A TROUBLED FAMILY IF THE VARIOUS MEMBERS ARE ALSO INVOLVED WITH ONE ANOTHER IN A FAMILY BUSINESS, BECAUSE ECONOMIC RELATIONSHIPS OFTEN LOCK INTO THE PERSONAL INTERDEPENDENCIES. THIS MAY BE A MAJOR REASON FAMILY BUSINESS RARELY LAST MORE THAN A FEW GENERATIONS. BUT EVEN WHERE THERE IS LITTLE OR NO PERSONAL FAMILY INVOLVEMENT, WORK SYSTEMS THAT DEAL WITH THE BASIC STRESSES OF LIFE, PARTICULARLY MEDICAL OR LAW PARTNERSHIPS, LABOR UNIONS, PSYCHIATRIC CLINICS, OR HOSPITALS AND TO SOME LESSER EXTENT SCHOOL SYSTEMS (BUT ESPECIALLY PRIVATE SCHOOLS), ALL HAVE RULES THAT GOVERN WHO IN THE FAMILY IS LIKELY TO BECAME ILL. OF ALL WORK SYSTEMS, HOWEVER, THE ONE THAT FUNCTIONS MOST LIKE A FAMILY IS THE CHURCH OR SYNAGOGUE.*

Change is problematic when it influences the system of flow, or the process of doing the "same things (programs and ministries) over and over." It is common for church members and leaders to have a sense of disappointment when things do not go the way some folks expect things to go. When reviewing more specific challenges, for example; making major changes in the life of the church, planning, or addressing new ideas for growth, an assessment is always the best plan.

This author is an advocate of ***hope and justice*** in the community and seeks to ***restore relationships*** that are grounded on the principles of the Christian church, where folks can share their stories of ***peace, hope, and justice.***

Many folks are afraid to start a new project or program. Many new converts will only observe, but refuse to get involved, because of fear of reprisal. One of the driving concerns is the ability to trust one another in the church. ***Trust is a key word for any organization, group, team, or church community attempting to established relationships.*** In the process for change, ***trust is a power principle,*** and without trust, organizations will be limited in their achievements. Trust is the church's expectation. ***Trust protects the soul of the church from decay and destruction from within.***

In Phil. 1:27 KJV, Paul says, "Only let your conversation be as it becomes the gospel of Christ." Although Paul was referring primarily to the Philippians' moral lives, his words also apply to church practices. Let them be worthy of the gospel of Christ. The spiritual test, however, is to build relationships that bring connectedness so that leaders will be more motivated to be active in the work of the true believers of Jesus Christ will be more active in developing one another as believers in the community. The challenge is for pastors of family churches to ***foster an environment of change in their churches while developing lasting relationships within the context of the local church.***

TOWARD A PARADIGM: A METHOD

CHAPTER THREE

The paradigm is a method on the premise that the church of Jesus Christ represents the ***values of unity, and genuine relationship.*** The history of new church development is unique and developing the congregation for community development and change is a new learning approach. ***In "From Typical Church to Social Ministry: A Study of the Elements Which Mobilize Congregations," Carl S. Dudley provides insights on the guiding principles that have shaped his work. The work of H. Paul Douglass created a time of immense possibility.***

Douglass first influenced this author when his church used ***Douglass' approach*** to help congregations adapt their programs and denominations to meet the challenge of changing social conditions.

When Douglass entered professional life at the turn of the century, he employed the sociology he learned from the University of Iowa, Columbia University, and the University of Chicago to address the problems confronting churches. Along with his field notes and interviews, Douglass was the first to make extensive use of survey methods and demographic data in both church and community analysis. Even with his pioneering work, though studied and reprinted by university sociologists, he felt unable to break into the tight circles of denominational decisionmaking or the glacial traditions of theological education.

Change and relationship building are needed in the lives of mainline, protestant, and black churches. ***In his book, Studying Congregations: A New Handbook, Dr. Carl Dudley asserts:***

> ***THEOLOGY CAN BE THE SPRINGBOARD FOR SPIRITUAL RENEWAL AND REVITALIZATION OF A CONGREGATION. THEOLOGY CAN HELP CONGREGATIONS MEET CHANGE NOT ONLY IN A WAY MORE FAITHFUL TO THEIR TRADITIONS AND ASPIRATIONS, BUT PROACTIVELY AND PROPHETICALLY IF THAT IS GOD'S CALL TO THEM.***

With respect to the book, research and literary reviews raise three areas for consideration: ***(1) Change is problematic, (2) Change is slow and long term and (3) working relationships are important to the church.***

The critiques of the resources are interrelated in the study of congregations with emphasis on spirituality and community development within the church. The resources share a common interest toward change. One of the greatest responsibilities of the church is change and developing leaders for church growth.

This author is convinced that people seeking spiritual direction must understand that the Judeo-Christian tradition holds up one imperative that summarizes all the principles of ethical and righteous living: in all circumstances, per ***Deut. 6:5(TEV) we are called to "love God with all of our heart, mind, and strength."*** Helping others live by the ***"Golden Rule"*** is an ethical responsibility.

Becoming spiritual is more than just reading Bible verses; it is a holistic development of oneself and others. Churches must provide supportive and challenging opportunities in which persons and the people of God can explore their relationships with God and others as they embark on their spiritual reflection and journey.

In the book, mighty like a River: The Black Church and Social Reform, Andrew Billingsley suggests that when people are not spirit-filled and connected, something is lost. The lack of getting involved leaves a congregation unable to function as an active people of God. ***Billingsley asserts, "We have found in our studies and observation that churches without dynamic and spirit-filled worship programs are not likely to sustain active community building activities. The two seem to reinforce each other."***

One of the unique aspects involved with this is addressing a model for the dynamics of change and building relationships that is ***grounded in compassion.*** In the article, ***"Saving Souls, Saving Society: Exploring the Spiritual and Social Dynamics of Church-Based Community Activism," Heidi Rolland Unruh and Ronald J. Sider asserts, "Spiritual outreach is grounded in social compassion because of the urgent immediate and long-term needs of their target population." The authors further add, "A different social context might engender a different expression of their mission, one lay leader suggested. The primary number one mission for Christians is to tell other people about Christ. [There are] a lot of different options we have of how to do it."***

Around adult learning, the research is clearly defined on the importance of learning and informing the congregation on faith in practice. In another study cited in the ***Journal of Spirituality, Growth, and Transformation, Elizabeth Price asserts: "These congregations risked naming and examining their own assumptions. These congregations were encouraged to think theologically, to engage metaphor and scripture and to develop symbols."***

In an article, ***"From Individual to Corporate Praxis: A Systemic Re-imagining of Religious Education," Barbara J. Fleischer of the Loyola University of New Orleans provides meaningful literature***

on congregational learning. Fleischer asserts that in 1990, Peter Senge opened the floodgates of new research and writing on learning organizations by introducing the discipline of shared vision through community. She further adds, "Senge also advocates an emphasis on team learning in the praxis movements of organization life. In teams (or in congregational life, communities), members in dialogue begin learning and thinking together with respect to the issues and challenges they must face in actualizing their mission and vision." There are five specific essential disciplines for organizations. The second most important discipline is the ***element of change*** and learning how to build a ***shared vision through community.*** The last author of which the researcher has determined based on the model of ministry is the idea of ***corporate learning.*** This concept is the heart of the researcher's model of ministry to bring about a ***"systems thinking" process.*** Senge writes:

> ***THE PRACTICE OF SHARED VISION INVOLVES THE SKILLS OF UNEARTHING SHARED "PICTURES OF THE FUTURE" THAT FOSTER GENUINE COMMITMENT AND ENROLLMENT RATHER THAN COMPLIANCE. IN MASTERING THIS DISCIPLINE, LEADERS LEARN THE COUNTER PRODUCTIVENESS OF TRYING TO DICTATE A VISION, NO MATTER HOW HEARTFELT.***

Senge's research is coupled with his work as an organizational consultant, primarily working out of the Massachusetts Institute of Technology Sloan School of Management. Senge's and his associates developed processes to help a variety of business, education, and service organizations learn the critical skills to clarify their collective optimal vision for future ***work on building community.*** This author's literary reviews on learning is noted by Timothy Lines. The author asserts further:

> ***The advantage of using the learning organizations disciplines as a conceptual framework for religious education is that they offer a more specific approach to systemic learning than the general principles offered by Timothy Lines, although Lines' work clearly outlines the implication of "system thinking" for religious education.***

The final constructive research that supports this researcher's ability to get the congregation involved is the ***Alan Institute publication by Gilbert R. Rendle*** who provided information on the dynamics of change with the idea of leaders working for change. He suggested that:

> ***Congregational change does not happen by gathering the larger circles of active, inactive, or community members and offering education or training. Change begins at the heart of the congregation, within the leadership circle. Leaders need to do the hard and necessary up-front work to understand and develop their own spirits, thoughts, and behaviors, which provide the health and the strength that will enable the congregation to live well with the stresses and demands of change.***

Rendle documents the response to congregational dynamics of change and behaviors as "sameness." ***Rendle*** is radical in his approach to helping leaders change. Changing the way, a congregation thinks and behaves is not a quick and easy exercise for leaders because it means wrestling with ***learned behaviors that people often practice without thinking.***

To such a degree, changing the feelings and behaviors of a congregation is changing the culture of the congregation, for organizational culture is based on assumptions of the organization given it identity and purpose. In the article entitled, ***"Rethinking Faith Formation" by Sondra Higgins, she reveals the importance of Christians building relationships that bring meaning, purpose, and direction.***

Higgins argues that a faith community's role is to participate in God's work by creating an intentional process of coming to know oneself as a Christian, having assimilated the values, beliefs, and lifestyle of one who professes a follower of Jesus Christ. ***Higgins*** argues that the aim of faith formation is a deepening relationship with God, or what some would call ***"spirituality,"*** and the faithful witness of word and action that grows out of this relationship. Relationships in the church or community are also important because they ***bring people together to achieve a common goal.***

With respect to the black church on the capacity to change, there is an appreciation of how a contingent value functions within the black church community. In an article entitled, ***"Understanding the Black Church: The Dynamics of Change," Douglas and Hopson asserts:***

> ***THE CHANGE PROCESS, THEREFORE, MUST ADDRESS THE ROLE THAT THIS VALUE PLAYS IN THE ENTIRE LIFE OF BLACK PEOPLE. THUS, A VARIETY OF EXPERTISE IS NEEDED TO ACCOMPLISH VIABLE CHANGE (I.E., SOCIOLOGICAL, PSYCHOLOGICAL, AND ANTHROPOLOGICAL, AS WELL AS THEOLOGICAL EXPERTISE).***
>
> ***FURTHER:***
>
> ***GIVEN THE BLACK CHURCH'S FUNDAMENTAL CONSERVING QUALITY, IT DOES NOT EASILY ACCOMMODATE CHANGE. AS BOTH A SOCIAL AND RELIGIOUS CENTER, IT HOLDS FAST TO WHAT WORKS. THE STRUCTURES, SYSTEMS, AND VALUES THAT ARE PERCEIVED TO BENEFIT BLACK SOCIAL, PHYSICAL, MENTAL, EMOTIONAL, AND SPIRITUAL HEALTHCARE VIRTUALLY INTRACTABLE.***

This author's research is consistent on the engagement of congregation learning combined with helping people understand themselves as proactive leaders in the church. Another example of engaging community within the tradition of the church is a systems approach to pastoral leadership. ***Mansell*** outlines four areas of congregational acceptance in which the director or leader will negotiate group dynamics to bring about ***unity, harmony, and the development of building community*** within the church or group process. It is in the key word, ***negotiation,*** a word that represents the intricate nature of the unending interaction between a pastor and congregation, which leads to leader acceptance. ***Patterson's four stages of acceptance are pictured in terms of a movement from "forming," to "storming," to "norming," to "performing."***

The four stages of change are as follows:

Stage 1 is ***STORMING***. In this stage, you have a group of individuals not yet systemically related to one another, except on an ad hoc basis. They are just getting together. The pastor is off to one side existentially and emotionally. The group may have called the pastor to serve it or to serve with it. Acceptance is pending. The system is not yet for the leader. The group has not yet given the leader full authority. The congregation does not yet manifest the properties of wholeness, cooperation, and isomorphism. Basically, the pastor is functioning to bring the group together at stated times---Christian service, a Bible study, prayer, or worship. That is all that is happening. A pastor in this new position should listen, observe, and not start many new things. It is probably wise for the pastor to do little that

> is new in a first year of ministry, except that which the people themselves might want to initiate.
>
> Stage 2 is ***Forming***. In this stage, the congregation moves toward forming its own identity and purpose. Having a new leader, the congregation is moving toward the formation of a new system. Between pastor and people there is a growing sense of common identity and shared goals, yet the pastor-leader is still perceived as an outsider, as a person negotiating the way "in." It is a strange paradox: The church is forming as much by the leader's function as by its own; yet, it is still holding the pastor at arm's length.

This stage is called storming because the new pastor-leader is a ***"disturbance"*** in the group. The pastor's presence introduces ***different paradigms*** that have not yet been realized. ***Patterson*** explains the third stage as follows:

> Stage 3 is ***Norming***. Problems in the journey to commonality become evident. What happens? The shared identity and common purpose requires each person to contribute in the same way. This has the effect of blocking individuality, an often-stressful experience for many Western people. As the congregation gets down to work, members feel a heightened tension between personal selffulfillment and the church's corporate achievement. Some members, protesting the "tyranny of the group," assert their individual identity. Some of these "deviants" may withdraw from the church to protest their own individual freedoms. Sometimes the church excludes them, and conflict ensues.

Building community is a continuous process with a variety of signature people, including the congregation, family, peers, and a combination of factors that are hidden from view and ever for discussion.

The researcher is also concerned with literature regarding the relationship between the ***churches spiritual nurture and the social activism as it relates to change. An article entitled, "Saving Souls, Saving Society: The Role of Evangelism in Church-Based Social Ministries,"*** provides three specific positive areas to review, as follows:

1. *Agency*: What is believed to come about through evangelism and/or social ministry, or what desired outcomes are associated with each? Some of the possibilities: Doing social ministry leads to opportunities for evangelism; only spiritual change makes social change possible; spiritual nurture and social activism together are necessary to build up the church as an alternative community of peace and injustice; or evangelism and social ministry have no consequential connection.

2. *Motivation*: What reasons do people give for being involved in outreach? Are the goals spiritual and/or social? For some, seeing people, come to Jesus is their greatest reward; others are motivated by seeing a homeless family housed. Others derive personal motivation and a pattern for service from their own experience of spiritual and/or social deliverance. Someone who has had a lifechanging conversion experience is more likely to incorporate an evangelistic emphasis into his or her ministry.

3. ***Theology/Worldview:*** How are evangelistic and social ministries related in the church's theological principles,

their use of Scripture, or their fundamental worldview (their understanding of nature of persons and spiritual/social realities)? What influences or models (besides Scripture) shape this understanding of the relationship between evangelism and social outreach? A church may defend the primacy of evangelism based on the Great Commission, go into all the world and make disciples; or it may model its understanding of ministry after Jesus, who came both to preach the Good News to the poor and set free the oppressed; or it may claim a historic legacy of championing the cause of social justice, based on a world view in which personal well-being is linked not only (or primarily) to individual spirituality, but to the struggle for group rights.

The paradigm method is created out of understanding the importance of relationships. This author asserts there are four specific assumptions for this book:

1. Congregations need to seek new opportunities for learning without following old rules. This assumption helps explore ways of addressing the issue of change with the ability to reflect, connect, and decide and to do. Congregational members and leaders learn best when they are doing something that reflects on what they just completed or what they learned. This opportunity to learn in community builds the best fellowship among members.

2. Change produces "heart feelings," which is good and not to be avoided. Working with different ideas that produce conflict is good in a time of change. If the congregation and the lay folks have only one idea, trying to do something different is difficult.

3. The congregation needs to appreciate experimentation. Learning requires the hard work of analysis, discussion, and discernment. Learning requires the willingness to experiment with new programs and new approaches that will provide new information, which will in turn achieve community among its members.

4. Leadership is a spiritual reality in the church or congregation. The congregation or church must move and find its relationships within its tradition and in the changed lives of its members. Leaders and lay folks have a crucial responsibility of building relationships and community to be effective stewards of Christ's service.

This approach is basic to developing leaders and good working relationships so that folks can respect the rights of others and trust one another. When relationships are formed, people begin to remember stories that bring a sense of connectedness to one another. Ultimately, a model for building relationships among congregates is to articulate a sense of purpose and connectedness. Finally, trust is the key to bringing about lasting working relationships where positive change can take place.

There are several working principles unique to this model, taken from ***Dr. Robert Rogers:***

THESE PRINCIPLES ON BELIEVING ARE COMMON TO CHURCH MEMBERS (1) HAVE A DEEP DESIRE TO MAKE A DIFFERENCE; (2) CAN BE TRUSTED TO MAKE THE RIGHT DECISIONS; (3) HAVE GENUINELY WORTHWHILE IDEAS; (4) WILL ENTHUSIASTICALLY RESPOND TO THE OPPORTUNITY FOR PERSONAL INVOLVEMENT WHEN THEY SEE THE DECIDING FOCUS OF MINISTRY; (5) HAVE THE MOST DIRECT KNOWLEDGE OF MINISTRY NEEDS AND CHALLENGES; AND (6) WORK

BEST WHEN TEAMED UP WITH OTHER MEMBERS WHO HAVE SIMILAR INTERESTS AND PASSIONS.

Dr. Saul Trinidad, Hispanic Lay Theology, depicts one of the major aspects to relationships and change. African American churches located in Hispanic and Latino communities need to address the complex problem of building relationships with folks from third-world countries. ***The National Plan,*** implemented by the United Methodist Church, developed a training program for Hispanic leadership.

The aim, per ***Dr. Trinidad, is "to help make possible a new way of being the church: a dynamic, growing church, as in the days of Pentecost; a church fully incarnated in the Hispanic context; and a church with a holistic ministry."*** Consequently, ***Dr. Trinidad assures that "in preparing the didactic sources materials, care has been taken to consider the experiences, knowledge and the academic level of most the Hispanic laity."***

Author Edgar H. Schein, in his work entitled, ***Organizational Culture,*** introduces a dynamic change model, comprised of five specific steps: (1) specifying goals, (2) comparing the present status with the first ideal, (3) dealing with tension, (4) developing a plan for change and (5) revisiting goals and the vision to count the cost of the new plan. Conflict around change comes when tension is not resolved in a productive way. He also states that the process of acknowledging tension by:

> ***UNFREEZING, OR CREATING A MOTIVATION TO CHANGE…IS, OF NECESSITY, COMPOSED OF THREE VERY DIFFERENT PROCESSES, EACH OF WHICH (EMPHASIS MINE) MUST BE PRESENT TO A CERTAIN DEGREE FOR THE SYSTEM TO DEVELOP ANY MOTIVATION TO CHANGE: 1) ENOUGH DISCONFIRMING DATA TO CAUSE SERIOUS DISCOMFORT AND DISEQUILIBRIUM; 2) THE CONNECTION OF THE DISCONFIRMING***

DATA TO IMPORTANT GOALS AND IDEALS CAUSING ANXIETY AND OR GUILT; AND 3) ENOUGH PSYCHOLOGICAL SAFETY, IN THE SENSE OF SEEING A POSSIBILITY OF SOLVING THE PROBLEM WITHOUT LOSS OF IDENTITY OR INTEGRITY.

However, the method for change and relationships or connecting with folks must reach at the core value of change for the good of the community. One's spiritual nurture and Christian living helps others work through issues to address issues in the local church.

This author also believes that working through a process of change for the good of the churches is healthy and will develop new sound leadership. As Christian workers and leaders, we often speak about change on a broader scale. Our local church community may need to change its views or move in a different direction for the future of others.

SUMMARY

Systems are changing and the ability to ***"make all things new"*** can and will succeed when unity of purpose is achieved. This may be problematic for those seeking not to change and make a difference in the lives of the congregation and themselves as lay leaders in the family of God. Proactive change and having positive relationships through an active engagement moves toward what God expects of those entrusted in his care.

CORE FOUNDATIONS

CHAPTER FOUR

This chapter contains a review of the theological, biblical, and historical perspectives associated with this author's view for developing opportunities for positive change and building relationships.

A review of the theologies is critical to the African American life. The works of ***Dr. James Cone*** and many other theologians have given rise to ***liberation and faith.*** A review of ***womanish theology*** is also necessary to systematic change in the lives of women and in the ministry of the church. ***Professional women in music have also contributed greatly to the cause of change and relationships.***

In his book, ***God of the Oppressed, James H. Cone*** affirms his statement of what black theology is:

> ***BLACK THEOLOGY IS A THEOLOGY OF AND FOR BLACK PEOPLE. IT IS AN EXAMINATION OF THEIR STORIES, TALES, AND SAYINGS. IT IS AN INVESTIGATION OF THE MIND INTO THE RAW MATERIALS OF OUR PILGRIMAGE, TELLING THE STORIES OF "HOW WE GOT OVER." FOR***

THEOLOGY TO BE BLACK, IT MUST REFLECT UPON WHAT IT MEANS TO BE BLACK. BLACK THEOLOGY MUST UNCOVER THE STRUCTURES AND FORMS OF THE BLACK EXPERIENCES, BECAUSE THE CATEGORIES OF INTERPRETATION MUST ARISE OUT OF THE THOUGHT FORMS OF THE BLACK EXPERIENCE ITSELF.

Paulo Freire asserts in Pedagogy of the Oppressed: "One of the gravest obstacles to the achievement of liberation is that oppressive reality absorbs those within it and thereby acts to submerge human beings' consciousness." Pedagogy of the Oppressed, which is the pedagogy of people engaged in the fight for their own liberation, has its roots here. Those who recognize, or begin to recognize, themselves as oppressed must be among the developers of this pedagogy. The challenge of the 21st century will be to develop a methodology that helps the ***"least of our community."*** In his book, ***Heart and Head, Dwight Hopkins*** pointed out that black theology has a faith connection. ***Hopkins asserts, "Based on the Christian scripture, the progressive sector of the African American church, for which a black theology speaks, maintains a subversive faith in Jesus Christ's spirit."***

Dr. Hopkins provides an accurate account of black theology when he says, ***"Black theology spiritual practice fundamentally means social transformation of wicked structures and destructive systems that hold a boot to the necks of the poor blacks in the United States."***

After a review of the theologies that affect the poor and the oppressed, the local church needs to evaluate its options for equipping the saints of God. Per ***Dr. Hopkins,*** we need to foster an attitude of social empowerment for equipping congregations toward a radical and progressive theology. First, the researcher will reflect on thè three vital theologies that appeal to the circumstances of the poor and the oppressed, which include; black theology, liberation theology and womanish theology. Finally, the exploration of these theologies in the context of the African American urban parish will give new understanding of equipping those to explore CORE foundations.

As one appreciates the value of the human spirit, applying theology of humanity is essential to understanding the poor and the oppressed with the idea of social change. African American and other liberation theologians from around the world have defined ***"structures and systems of oppression, degradation, and marginalization,"*** and ***"African American and other liberation theologians have emphasized inherent human dignity and its diminishment through structures and systems of oppression, degradation, and marginalization."*** They argue that the struggle against oppression and for liberation is religious as well as sociopolitical. This struggle for "full humanity" demonstrates and restores human dignity, not only for the oppressed, but also for the oppressor, whose ***"humanity is diminished by participation in and collusion with domination."***

A central strategy for social transformation and change is essential in the face of the problems associated with poverty, the poor, and the oppressed. In a time of rapid social change, there is intense interest in what it means to be human or humane. The doctrine of humanity, therefore, "addresses a question of potentially greater interest than any other area in theology."

In the twentieth century, black theologies in American arose from the context of the civil rights black power movement. This was consistent with the history of blacks in America, shaped by the experiences of slavery, discrimination, and injustice. ***James Evans in his book, We Have Been Believers, asserts:***

> ***BLACK RELIGION HAS ALWAYS CONCERNED ITSELF WITH THE FASCINATION OF AN INCORRIGIBLY RELIGIOUS PEOPLE WITH THE MYSTERY OF GOD, BUTT HAS BEEN EQUALITY CONCERNED WITH THE YEARNING OF A DESPISED AND SUBJUGATED PEOPLE FOR***

> ***FREEDOMFREEDOM FROM THE RELIGIOUS, ECONOMIC, SOCIAL, AND POLITICAL DOMINATION THAT WHITES HAVE EXERCISED OVER BLACKS SINCE THE BEGINNING OF THE AFRICAN SLAVE TRADE.***

It is important to understand black theology from the perspective of the oppressed and the poor. The ***social gospel*** had an impact on the lives of people and society needed a change for the good of humanity. Black theology is a challenge to the status symbols of society and addresses the political and social ills of our society. In his book, ***A Theology for the Social Gospel, Walter Rauschenbusch states:***

> ***THE SOCIAL MOVEMENT IS THE MOST IMPORTANT ETHICAL AND SPIRITUAL MOVEMENT IN THE MODERN WORLD AND THE SOCIAL GOSPEL IS THE RESPONSE OF THE CHRISTIAN CONSCIOUSNESS TO IT. THE SOCIAL GOSPEL IS THE OLD MESSAGE OF SALVATION, BUT ENLARGED AND INTENSIFIED. THE INDIVIDUALISTIC GOSPEL HAS TAUGHT US TO SEE THE SINFULNESS OF EVERY HUMAN HEART AND HAS INSPIRED US WITH FAITH IN THE WILLINGNESS AND POWER OF GOD TO SAVE EVERY SOUL THAT COMES TO HIM.***

This author's view is that black theology and the social gospel seek to bring men and women under the repentance for the wrongs of society and the suffering of generations.

Black theology can and must address the problems associated with poverty, the poor and the oppressed. It must be both prophetic and liberated in its efforts. The ideas of justice and hope are related in the theme of relationship and allowing people to free in their thoughts and have a community of faith.

Theologically, God's love is prior to the other themes. To separate love in the context of black religion from a similar theme in white religion, however, it is important to emphasize that love in black religion is usually linked with ***God's justice and hope. "God's love is made known through divine righteousness, liberating the poor for a new future."*** One of the driving themes of the liberation of black theology is hope. In an article entitled, ***"Calling the Oppressors to Account: Justice, Love, and Hope in Black Religion," James Cone asserts: "The theme of justice is closely related to the idea of hope. The God who establishes the right and puts down the wrong is the sole basis of the hope that the suffering of the victims will be eliminated."***

Black theologies are connected to the Christian message of Jesus Christ and to God's work of deliverance. African American people should review where they are in the struggle for justice and hope. Black, liberation and womanish theologies speak of hope and liberation. ***James Cone asserts:***

> ***BLACK THEOLOGY MUST TAKE SERIOUSLY TWO REALITIES, TWO ASPECTS OF A SINGLE REALITY: THE LIBERATION OF BLACKS AND THE REVELATION OF JESUS CHRIST. FOR THESE TWO REALITIES FORM THE NORM OF A BLACK THEOLOGY: THE NORM OF ALL GOD-TALK WHICH SEEKS TO BE BLACK-TALK IS THE MANIFESTATION OF JESUS AS THE BLACK CHRIST WHO PROVIDES THE NECESSARY SOUL FOR BLACK LIBERATION."***

One of the aspects of supporting the local church in a strategy for social change for the poor and the oppressed is the understanding of scripture within a black theology. Despite all the theologies in question, black theology is grounded in biblical scripture and is the cornerstone of faith.

SCRIPTURE IN BLACK THEOLOGY

Throughout the life of the late ***Dr. Martin L. King, Jr,*** the writings of ***Walter Rauschenbusch*** and the social gospel movement influenced King. ***Rauschenbusch*** stressed the prophetic model of religion with a public stand against injustice and immorality. The public evil of millions of poor people and the evil societal condition of poverty is sinful and oppressive. ***Dr. King*** was greatly influenced by ***Rauschenbusch's work*** and his deep concern for the poor. What deeply inspired king he studied and experienced; for example, King's study on the Hebrew prophets and scripture is related to the Sermon on the Mount and the ***Beatitudes in Matthew, chapter 5, NASB:***

> *Blessed are the poor in spirit, for theirs is the kingdom of heaven. Blessed are those who mourn, for they will be comforted. Blessed are the meek, for they shall inherit the earth. Blessed are those who hunger and thirst for righteousness, for they shall be filled. Blessed are the merciful, for they shall obtain mercy. Blessed are the pure in heart, for they shall see God. Blessed are the peacemakers, for they shall be called sons of God. Blessed are those who are persecuted for righteousness' sake, for theirs is the kingdom of heaven (Matt. 5:3-11 NASB).*

Dr. Martin L. King, Jr., repeatedly quoted the famous passage from ***Amos 5:24 NASB:***

"But let judgment run down as waters, and righteousness as a mighty stream." Scripture is a biblical hermeneutic for change and in the experience of black theology, equipping the local church for action.

The biblical stories and scriptural passages that have historically found their way into black preaching are those that have clearly demonstrated the mighty acts of God on behalf of people, whom were in situations of powerlessness consistent with, though different from, those of the forcibly displaced Africans in America. Stories, as well as other passages of scripture, that speak of the mighty acts of God ***on behalf of the marginalized*** initially attracted blacks to the God of the Christian religion during the days of slavery. "Black folks embraced this God by the thousands in the eighteenth and nineteenth centuries after hearing the good news of God's promise of salvation from sin and death, but also after hearing of what God had done for the oppressed in biblical times."

The theme of justice and Yahweh's special concern for the poor and the widows has a central place in Israelite prophecy per ***Dr. James Cone.*** In the book of Jeremiah, for example:

For among my people there are wicked men,
their houses are full of fraud, as a cage is full of birds.
They grow rich and grand, bloated and rancorous;
their thoughts are all of evil, and they refuse to do justice,
the claims of the orphan they do not put right
nor do they grant justice to the poor
(Jer. 5:26-28 NEB).

CONE ASSERTS:

The emphasis upon justice for the poor is present even in a prophet like Isaiah of Jerusalem, for whom David's reign, rather than the Exodus, is the significant act of deliverance. Per Isaiah, "Yahweh bound himself by a covenant oath to David, promising to preserve the Davidic line to spare the Davidic kingdom for the sake of my servant David'... (Isa. 37:35, see II Sam. 7)."

Dr. Cone makes it clear in almost every scene of the Old Testament drama of salvation; the poor are defended against the rich, the weak against the strong. Yahweh is the God of the oppressed whose revelation is identical with their liberation from bondage. Even in the wisdom literature, where the sages seem to be unaware of Israel's saving history, God's concern for the poor is nonetheless emphasized:

He who is generous to the poor lends to the Lord (Prov. 19:17 NEB).

He who oppresses the poor insults his Maker; he who is generous to the needy honors him (Prov. 14:13 NEB).

Black theology addresses the poor and Yahweh's own, his special possession. These are the people that the Divine has called into being for freedom. God, or Yahweh, judges the Israelites based on how they treat the poor. The formal accusation is hard, painful, and severe:

The Lord comes forward to argue his case and stands to judge his people. The Lord opens the formal accusation against the elders of his people and their officers: They have ravaged the vineyard, and the spoils of the poor are in your houses. Is it nothing to you that you crush my people and grind the faces of the poor? (Isa. 3:13-15 NEB)

J. Deotis Roberts has written of the theological significance of scripture for black theology:

> ***The Bible, for blacks, is a "living book." Recognition of the creative and providential involvement of God in the history of the people of the Old Testament is basic to black interpretation. A direct relationship through faith exists between God's acts of liberating Israel and the freedom struggle of blacks. In black theology, there is no "quest" for the historical Jesus. Jesus is present as a Divine Friend. The prophet speaks for God in judgment against the dehumanization of the poor and the weak. However, there is also an awareness of sin and guilt and the need for forgiveness among blacks. Black theology also recognizes God's forgiveness of the oppressor who meets God's demands for justice and love toward the needy and the helpless. This is not "cheap grace," for it includes the acceptance of the dignity and equality of all human beings and the sharing of power.***

In the last forty years, black theology has attempted to serve as the biblical hermeneutic for black liberation and for the black church. Along with ***James Cone, J. Deotis Roberts and Dwight Hopkins*** are viewed as the indisputable progenitors of the academic communities, supporting local congregations to identify the need for change. Leaders of local congregations are challenged to address issues of the poor and the oppressed. ***Forrest Harris*** provides yet another view that supports a constructive theology of the oppressed viewing the black church as a method for social change and transformation. He brings the community and church together through theological reflection and social analysis when he asserts:

> ***The task of every Christian is to do theology in terms of seeking to understand how God acts in history and in the life of the community. Black theology affirms that the "black experience" of survival and liberation are in solidarity with the redemptive and liberating acts of God. The task, then, of black theology is to interpret how God is a concrete part of the black experience and to articulate the conditions of God's involvement in the experience.***

This author's view is that womanist theology can speak to change in holistic values. Womanist theology alongside is an effective strategy of black liberation. Black women theologians like: ***Katie Cannon, Jacquelyn Grant, Delores Williams, Kelly Brown Douglas, Marcia, Cheryl Townsend Gilkes, Cheryl Sanders, Linda Thomas, and others represent prophetic voices of hope for the poor and the oppressed of the black community.***

Pulitzer Prize-winning novelist Alice Walker and others encourage womanist theology. Walker coined the term ***"womanish"*** in her 1983 book ***In Search of Our Mother's Gardens,*** when she said, "You are acting womanish." Per Walker, this means ***"wanting to know more and in greater depth than is good for one...outrageous, audacious, courageous, and willful behavior."***

Womanist theology is a ***theology of empowerment*** and seeks to bring about a holistic perspective with a concern for the suffering and celebration of others. Per ***Katie G. Cannon:***

> ***The focus of womanish ethics is on justice for women, survival and "a productive quality of life for poor women,***

> *CHILDREN AND MEN." THIS MEANS THE WOMANISH THEOLOGIAN "MUST GIVE AUTHORITATIVELY STATUS TO BLACK FOLK WISDOM (E.G., BRER RABBIT LITERATURE) AND TO BLACK WOMEN'S MORAL WISDOM (EXPRESSED IN THEIR LITERATURE) WHEN SHE RESPONDS TO THE QUESTION, "HOW OUGHT THE CHRISTIAN TO LIVE IN THE WORLD?"*

Womanist theology can and will play a vital role in equipping the local church to address those issues of ***empowerment and the celebration*** of the issues associated with African American women in the African American church and community. ***Cheryl Townsend Gilkes says in her book, "If wasn't For the Women":***

> *AMONG THE CRISES FACING AFRICAN AMERICANS TODAY AND ONE THAT IS FOLLOWING US INTO THE 21ST CENTURY, IS THE SITUATION OF POOR WOMEN IN OUR COMMUNITIES. FOLK WISDOM RECOGNIZES THE IMPORTANCE OF "THE MOTHERS" TO THE SURVIVAL AND HEALTH OF THE COMMUNITY AND TO THE PERPETUATION OF WORTHWHILE DIMENSIONS OF AFRICAN-AMERICAN CULTURE. CHRISTIAN MINISTRY IS DEFINED ULTIMATELY BY ITS SERVICE TO, WITH AND ON BEHALF OF "THE LEAST OF THESE."*

The local church can begin to address womanish issues like sexism and the treatment of black women, even in the church.

In a book, she edited, entitled, ***Living Stones in the Household of God: The Future of Black Theology, Dr. Linda Thomas asserts,*** "Womanist theology highlights the overlooked styles and contributions of all black women whether they are poor and perhaps illiterate, or economically advantaged and "PhD.'ed." ***Dr. Thomas furthers adds:***

AN ETHNOGRAPHIC METHODOLOGY NECESSITATES OUR ENTERING THE COMMUNITIES OF THESE WOMEN, CONSTITUTING FOCUS GROUPS, AND UTILIZING THEIR LIFE EXPERIENCES AS THE PRIMARY SOURCES FOR THE DEVELOPMENT OF QUESTIONS WHICH ESTABLISHED A KNOWLEDGE BASE FROM EVERYDAY PEOPLE.

Womanist theology and scripture are hopeful on linking the poor and the oppressed as a model to biblical understanding. It is linked to family and building relationships within the context of church, homes and in the corporate setting of society.

Black women hold the Bible as a major source of religious validation in their lives. Many women can see the stories of shame and pain, throughout it all, keep moving forward while trusting in their faith. Black women theologian can identify and reflect upon those biblical stories in which poor oppressed women had a special encounter with divine emissaries of God.

The story of Hagar in the book of Genesis, for example, is "***most illustrative and relevant to Afro-American women's experience of bondage, of African heritage, and of an encounter with God during fierce survival struggles.***"

In the New Testament, womanish theologians focus on the beginning of the salvation story when the Spirit comes upon Mary, a poor woman ***(Lk. 1:35). Luke 18: 1-6*** is a parable Jesus tells about a poor widow who continuously comes before an unjust male judge.

A womanist theology can bring about transformation in the life of people that struggle and need the nurture of well-educated and informed people of faith. Throughout history, we recognize the work of liberation and freedom for black women in our present age. Per Dr. ***Dwight Hopkins' book, Down, up and Over:***

> *The poor and brokenhearted are co-agents with divine intent to fashion a new emancipated human self. In a word, God works with us through the act of freedom, as we constitute ourselves from oppression to a full reality of the highest potential of a liberated humanity. God liberates us totally and holistically."*

Cheryl Sanders observes that the primary purposes of theology are the narratives, autobiographies, novels, poetry, prayers, and other writings that convey black women's traditions,
culture, and history:

> *The method developed to appropriate these sources can also be summarized in terms of its celebrative, critical, and constructive intent, inclusive of 1) the celebration of black women's historical struggles and strength; 2) the critique of various manifestations of black women's oppression in terms of race, class, and sex; and 3) the construction of black women's distinctive theological and ethical claims towards a liberated praxis.*

This author is convinced that liberation theologies can help identify issues appropriate to the African American context and raise awareness of the ***constant need for hope and positive relationships*** that are vital to the local church. The proposition of black theology, liberation theology and womanish theology is a constant reminder of how these theologies have taken root in our local congregations and how change and hope has taken place among these theologies.

BIBLICAL FOUNDATION

Dr. William R. Herzog, II, in his book Jesus, Justice, and the Reign of God, says: "Jesus criticizes them for tithing 'mint, dill, and cumin,' herbs not covered by tithing requirements, while neglecting 'the weightier matters of the law': justice and mercy and faith (Matt. 23:23a)."

Israel was to be the image and chosen people of God, exhibiting God's glory in love toward God and human beings. Loving one's neighbor meant making no class distinctions. The urban world of promised inheritance that the Israelites entered was a world of haves and have-nots; a class society of powerful and powerless; and ethnic divisions of insider, outsider, and stranger. Poverty and oppression were also enemies to overcome in the mission of a new community. The stated reality that there would always be poor people in the land only underlined Israel's calling to be "openhanded toward your brothers and toward the poor and needy," per ***Deut. 15:11.***

When looking at a biblical perspective or foundation for the poor and the oppressed, it is clear to this author that liberation justice is imperative in the Old and New Testament biblical readings. It is not enough, however, to say that God reveals Himself in history and that therefore Israel's faith fleshes out a historical framework. This is the meaning of Yahweh's interventions in history. ***The purpose of God's activity is not to demonstrate his power, but to liberate and make justice reign:***

> *Father of orphans, defender of widows Such is God in his holy dwelling; God gives the lonely a permanent home, makes prisoners happy by setting them free, but rebels must live in an arid land (Ps. 68:5-6 NRSV)*

The God of history and the God of biblical proclamation is a ***God of justice.*** His power is expressed in defending the rights of the poor:

> *Who executes justice for the oppressed, who gives food to the hungry? The Lord gives freedom to the prisoners. The Lord opens the righteous. The Lord watches over the stranger; He relieves the fatherless and widow; but the way of the wicked He turns upside down (Ps. 146:7-9 NRSV).*

The knowledge of God is love of God. In the language of the Bible, ***"to know"*** is not something purely intellectual. To ***"know"*** means to love. Sin is the absence of the knowledge of Yahweh and it is on this that the people will be judged, per ***Hos. 4:1 TEV:*** "Sons of Israel listen to the word of Yahweh, for Yahweh indicts the inhabitants of the country."

One of the greatest narratives of the Old Testament is Nehemiah's forward and positive efforts to build relationships and build the wall. He was a governor who not only had the heart of the people in the land of Judah, but also the hope of building relationships to complete the building of the wall. Throughout the six chapters of Nehemiah, he depended on God in his efforts to finish building the wall, even though the threat of being killed and stopping the work was upon him. ***Neh. 6:10-13 TEVsays:***

> *One day when I went into the house of Shemaiah son of Delilah son of Mehetabel, who was confined to his house, he said, "let us meet in the house of God, within the temple, and let us close the doors of the temple, for they are coming to kill you; indeed, tonight they are coming to kill you." But, I said, "Should a man like me run away? Would a man like me go into the temple to save his life? I will not go in!" Then I perceived and saw that God had not sent him at all, but he had pronounced the prophecy against*

> *me because Tobiah and Sanballat had hired him. He was hired for this purpose, to intimidate me and make me sin by acting in this way and so they could give me a bad name, to taunt me."*
> *(Neh. 6:10-13 TEV)*

To edifice relationships was important to the Nehemiah's success with God and his people. Nehemiah's confidence in God and the work of the faithful, the returning exiles began to believe and know that God is faithful. Relationships, however, are built with conversation; time spent together; and common faith, ***one word, one action and one gesture at a time.***

The ***prophet Amos*** was deeply concerned about the poor and their relationship with God. Our relationship with God is expressed in our relations with the poor. As ***Prov. 17:5 NKJV says,*** "He who mocks the poor reproaches his Maker." One important factor related to this Old Testament view is the covenant God made with Abraham. This covenant implies a ***double belonging*** per Gutierrez ***in his book, The Power of the Poor in History: Biblical Overview:***

> ***GOD TO THE JEWISH PEOPLE AND OF THE JEWISH PEOPLE TO GOD. THE GUARANTEE OF THIS MUTUAL POSSESSION IS YAHWEH'S LOVE, AS EXPRESSED IN THE DEED BY WHICH HE LIBERATED THE PEOPLE'S SERVITUDE IN EGYPT. YAHWEH DEMANDS IN EXCHANGE THAT THE PEOPLE BEAR WITNESS TO HIM IN HISTORY.***

The Exodus provides a perspective in which the covenant is situated, and the covenant gives full meaning to the liberation from Egypt. This is the process by which the "people of God" are built. To be just is to be faithful to the covenant. To be faithful to the covenant means to practice the justice implied in God's liberating activity on behalf of the oppressed. This practice of justice as an expression of fidelity is found in the promise that precedes the covenant struck with Abraham:

> *Now, Yahweh wondered, "Shall I conceal from Abraham what I am going to do, seeing that Abraham will become a great nation with all the other nations of the earth blessing themselves by him? For I have singled him out to command his sons and his household after him to maintain the way of Yahweh by just and upright living. In this way, Yahweh will carry out for Abraham what he has promised him (Gen. 18:17-19 NRSV).*

One of the central concerns of the New Testament church is Paul's concern for the poor and sharing the ***Good News.*** Taking the ***Good News*** to the Gentiles is bringing to them "the unsearchable riches of Christ," per ***Eph. 3:8 NIV.*** The call to conversion is a declaration of what God in Christ has done, is doing, and will do.

The urban lifestyle of Paul's New Testament world existed as a lifestyle of survival with the hope of a new direction and change. It was to be society's new direction, modeling before the city of God's divine intentions for his creation. Per ***Dr. Stambaugh's book, The New Testament in Its Social Environment:***

> *Repeatedly the church found itself at points of tension in cities divided socially, economically, and ethnically. At these points, the Church's calling was to demonstrate a new kind of community, one where rich and poor were to share hare the same table (1 Cor 11:18-22) and where runaway slaves became brothers (Philem. 15-16). In a society where the brutal disparities of power and the powerlessness, where political realities, the Christian community echoed with Paul and Jesus. "My grace is all you need, for my power is strongest when you are weak" (2 Cor. 12:9 TEV).*

In a ***top-down society*** where such standards as occupational prestige, income, education, and family position measured ranking, per ***Meeks in The First Urban Christians: The Social World of the Apostle Paul,*** the church found room for all, with a concern for those at the social ladder's bottom rung ***(1 Cor. 1:26-28).*** The Christian church is called to respond with a ***"can-do mentality."*** Paul's letters indicate that the churches had their share of well-to-do Christians who had benefited from the Lord's grace upon them.

The more we consider the New Testament, the more we see scriptures that address the issue of change. God's people were to be city lights shining before the Gentiles, "that they may see your good works and praise your Father in Heaven ***(Matt. 5:14-16TEV).***

Evidence is given to scholarship with compassion and reaching out into the city to those who are less fortunate is a superb effort. Per ***Ortiz in his book, Urban Ministry: The Kingdom, the City, and the People of God:***

> ***THE WELFARE OF THE CITY IN THE GRECO-ROMAN WORLD DEPENDED ON THE ONGOING CONTRIBUTIONS OF CIVIC-MINDED BENEFACTORS. THEY PAID FOR PUBLIC WORKS FROM THEIR PRIVATE RESOURCES TO ENHANCE THE ENVIRONS OF THEIR CITIES AND IN TIME OF FAMINE, TO ENSURE THE SUPPLY OF GRAIN AT A COST AFFORDABLE TO EVERY CITIZEN.***

At the heart of Paul's missionary method was his perspective on the history of redemption. God's new order had initiated through the coming of Christ and his death and resurrection. Through the coming of the Holy Spirit, a new age was being constructed while the old age still existed. The Jubilee day of salvation, the time of favor when God would restore the land ***(Isa. 49:8),*** was no longer a promissory note; it was ***"now."*** Paul affirmed that now ***"is the time of God's favor, now is the day of salvation" (2 Cor. 6:2NIRV).***

Upon the scattered house churches of the empire, ***"the fulfillment of the ages has come" (1 Cor. 10:11 NIV).*** Paul sees his own ministry as deeply linked to that eschatological day. It is embedded in his striking phrase of self-evaluation: ***"I have fulfilled the gospel of Christ" (Rom. 15:19 NIRV).*** The scope of Paul's geographical reference is "from Jerusalem all the way around Illyricum" and to the Gentile lands.

In the Hellenistic world, to speak of the inhabited world, the oikumene was to speak of the city. Paul has a mission to the Gentiles with a message of hope for the Gentiles are an act of worship and praise to God. Enriching and reshaping this doxology of worship and praise are the realities of the new covenant.

The Old Testament phrase for formal Israelite worship was ***"to call on the name of the Lord" (Gen. 4:26; 12:8, and 26:25 NKJV).*** In the coming day of the Lord, God would purify even the lips of ***"the peoples, that all of them may call on the name of the Lord" (Zep. 3:9 KJV).*** In fact, everything we do, whether in word or deed, is to be done ***"in the name of the Lord Jesus" (Col. 3:17 KJV).*** Israel's Tabernacle God has come to be with us and Immanuel/Jesus is his name ***(Matt. 1:12-23).***

The church is the body of Christ, that community in whom Christ dwells, turned outward in action toward the world in ***1 Cor. 12:12-27 KJV:***

> *For as the body is one, and hath many members, and all the members of that one body, being many are one body: so also, is Christ. For by one Spirit are we all baptized into one body, whether we be Jews or Gentiles, whether we be bond or free; and have been all made to drink into one Spirit. For the body is not one member, but many. If the foot shall say, because I am not the hand, I am not of the body; is it therefore not of the body? And if*

> *the ear shall say, because I am not the eye, I am not of the body; is it therefore not of the body? If the whole body were an eye, where was the hearing? If the whole were hearing, where was the smelling? But now hath God set the members every one of them in the body, as it hath God set the members every one of them in the body, as it hath pleased him (1 Cor. 12:12-27 KJV).*

Into the urban world came Jesus of Nazareth. Along with his coming came the inauguration of ***God's urban renewal plan.*** Babel's human quest for unity in rebellion is finally fulfilled in God's gift of unity in ***"one Lord, one faith, one baptism" (Eph. 4:5 KJV).*** On a stairway-tower God stood, promising blessing to a fleeting Jacob and all the families of the earth. Out of that site emerged a city, Bethel, "the house of God." Reflecting on that history, Jesus promises to Nathaniel that a new reality has surpassed Jacob's dream: You shall see heaven open, and the angels of God ascending and descending on the Son of Man ***(Jn. 1:51).*** Jesus is the stairway, that one in whom heaven comes down to the cities of the world and through whom we ascend to the heavenly city. After three days in the belly of the great fish, a reluctant Jonah went forth, virtually resurrected form the dead, to promise God's redemption to a repenting Nineveh. Jesus preaching, "something greater than Jonah," calls the cities to repentance. In addition, the sign of his grace and power will be upon the city and all those who witness Jonah's new ***spirit of renewal and change.***

Ezekiel spoke of the day when God himself would return to Zion and take up residence as its rightful king, when the Shekinah glory departed. At the center of this urban restoration, all the urban domains of royalty would be fulfilled in God. His would be the sacred city kingship "in the order of Melchizedek" ***(Gen. 14; Ps. 110:4 KJV).*** It is that end-time community which the Christ, in action as Spirit, forms and equips to continue His work of reconciling men in every city, village, and town of our time, reconciling them to God and one another.

What does it mean to reach out to the poor and the oppressed? This author believes that the church needs biblical understanding to reach out to the poor and the oppressed. The church has often been negligent in reaching the poor because its members are limited in their understanding of the great commission. God did not intend that there would be poor people in our cities. He desired Jerusalem to be "a city centered in the worship of God" and practicing what we preach and teach. ***Dr. Cone says in his book, God of the Oppressed:***

> ***If Jesus' life with the poor reveals that the continuity between the Old and New Testaments is found in the divine will to liberate the oppressed from sociopolitical slavery, what then is the discontinuity? Or, more appropriately, in what sense does the New Testament witness take us beyond the Old and fulfill it? The new element is this: the divine freedom revealed in Jesus, as that freedom is disclosed in the cross and resurrection, is more than the freedom made possible in history. While God's freedom for the poor is not less than the liberation of slaves from bondage (Exodus), yet it is more than that historical freedom.***

God wants justice for his people. Dr. Cone continues:

> ***Jesus' conquest of Satan and the demons also carries out the theme of the liberation of the poor. "If it is by the finger of God that I drive out the devils, then be sure that the kingdom of God has already come upon you" (Lk. 11:20 NEB). Jesus' power to exorcize demons is the sine qua non- of the appearance of the kingdom, because freedom for the***

> ***OPPRESSED CAN COME ABOUT ONLY BY OVERCOMING THE FORCES OF EVIL.***

In the Old Testament and the New Testament alike, God expresses profound concern for the poor and delivers scathing indictments of all who would oppress them. Today, we cannot pretend the poor do not exist. The churches have a biblical mandate and must take responsibility and reorder priorities to fulfill their moral and ethical responsibilities to the poor.

Dr. Dwight N. Hopkins, in his book Down, Up, and Over: Slave Religion and Black Theology, says: "The Spirit of liberation in us causes the bottom of society to fight to reconstitute so that the poor might have the life of their humanity made real." Dr. Hopkins further adds:

> ***THE POOR AND BROKENHEARTED ARE CO-AGENTS WITH THE DIVINE INTENT TO FASHION A NEW EMANCIPATED HUMAN SELF. IN A WORD, GOD WORKS WITH US THROUGH THE ACT OF FREEDOM AS WE CONSTITUTE OURSELVES FROM OPPRESSION TO A FULL REALITY OF THE HIGHEST POTENTIAL OF A LIBERATED HUMANITY.***

One of the most important aspects of this section is the impact on families and the black church. The diversified black family has its strengths and weaknesses. Unfortunately, there is a survival mode for the black family, where slavery's impact is clearly present. Historically the church and family have survived out of deprivation and oppression. It is imperative that black churches continue to develop opportunities for dialogue and build bridges within the local church among themselves. In the words of ***Dr. Wallace Charles Smith in his book, The Black Church: Facing the Crisis of Family Living:***

"Sadly, for many blacks, the secularization of the twentieth century has exacted a great price. The church no longer occupies the central position of authority in the life of blacks that it once did. This fact has a great impact on the families. Families that are most broken are the families who are at the lower end of the socioeconomic scale. Studies also indicate that it is primarily this group of the so-called underclass that is not being reached by churches.

In slavery and the slave system relationship, the only way African Americans could move forward was in how things were done. Relationships served as an important part of the black experience. In this context, the local church needs to value family as an intercultural relationship.

Finally, the theology discussed has a focus to the meaning of the church, community, and the pedagogical response to change. Creating change brings people to a better understanding on making the local open to new opportunities. For the study of New Testament is undergirding by conflict and the transformation of communities in reform. Historically and biblically, the stories of time can bring about healing with the contribution of folks addressing their joys, hopes and dream for those in the local church. Hence, the struggling church can challenge itself with lay leadership to address those issues of homeless, teenage displacement, education for the least of the community. There are many issues impacting aging and declining congregations lack the ability to address many of the conversations that are emotional and heard to address to its members of their church community. Until this idea or concept can change, leadership must have a conversation on issues that could threaten the integrative of the local church. the lay leadership must be able to challenge the issues that hinder change in the life of the congregation and the local community. After much consideration given to theoretical foundations, the spiritual vision helps to drive the possibility of positive relationships. ***Positive energy creates positive change.*** The vision is founded on our experiencing our creator as continually present to us, helping everyone realize our full potential as people of God and as participants in a process for improving relationships, roles, and life projects.

The researcher has a sense that personal identity and purpose must become a visible sign of those who are connected to positive change. It is only when compassionate believers can live out their purpose that consistently addresses the needs of the people that they can have the fortitude toward each other. As the body of Christ is actively involved, people share information more effectively and effective ministries begin to unfold.

The traditional church must be free to explore the narratives of the past to appreciate how God has blessed and provided the foundation for Christian service. This provides a framework for a purpose, mission, and goals. Clearly the theoretical foundation provides credibility to building relationships among people as it relates to customs, traditions, and the work of the church in our society. One question is to be asked, is what a congregation is. Maureen R. O'Brien in her article, how we are together: Educating for Group self-understanding in the congregation. ***O' Brien reflects that a congregation is a group associated as "community".*** The community will view themselves in terms of interpersonal bonding and care, using language strongly influenced by the tradition of their culture. She adds that congregation will also be likely to draw upon the elements of the faith tradition that support this understanding of community."

Maureen O'Brien, *How We Are Together Educating for Groups Self-Understanding in the Congregation,* Religious Education, The Congregation as Educator; Journal of the Religious Education Association and the Association of Professors and Researchers in Religious Education, Volume 92, Nu. 3, summer 1997, p.315

CONCLUSION

These theoretical foundations provide a fresh understanding on how history plays in the process of understanding the human condition. The human condition is blessed with literature that is historical, traditional, and contemporary. Literature informs the intellect, our emotions to think critically about to response to the issues impacting our daily life. My perspective how do we as the so called faithful "build those areas of ministry into a solid foundation for our political, economic and spiritual well bring. I believe the "church within the small African American communities such as the "family" need the education to develop leaderships for the next generation. ed all of us, on the perspective on how ***"people"*** respond to the scholarship on issues of social, political and the affairs of ***"human affairs.*** History helps a congregation to review what was and to discern, while moving forward into the future for the next generation of congregations. In a book entitled The Choice: Living Your Passion Inside Out, by Frank A. Thomas, I quote: "many people go through their lives being who they have always been, thinking what they have always thought, believing what they always believed, keeping the same friends they always kept, going to the same places they've always gone". ...The continue to say: "many people have never stretched and have never expanded." how to produce "good fruit" for the next generation. The past helps one understand the future and anticipate a positive future for generations to come. This chapter has discussed the unique power of survival of a people and how relationships at the core are grounded in a people to rise, while providing a critical review on centuries past.

Frank A. Thomas, The Choice: Living Your Passion Inside Out, (Hope for International Books: 2013) p.105

REFLECTIONS AND CONCLUSIONS

CHAPTER FIVE

The theme surrounding this book is ***Urban Development and Intercultural Communication.*** Communication is one of the resources that is limited in the life of the Church. Communication is an urgent task to address the most unique areas of conflict, change and the future of the congregation. Communication leads to an upward bound to new area of conversation and it also my hope is that the focus of this book brings the power of community and a new perspective toward ministry at the forefront of the change that needs to take place.

The book served as an effort of this author's personal growth experience. Through the efforts of general ministry of those that engage ministry as local pastor, the ability to be a servant requires the ability to address the ***"supervisory concept of ministry".*** Doctors of the church must understand the ***role of supervision.*** Supervising those that are involved in ministry in the local church and addressing the issues that impact the lives of all, involved in transformation of our community. Finally, this writer has grown toward the conviction on the implementation of ***a ministry model that meets the need of the local church***, rather than simply preaching, and teaching the Gospel of peace.

Ministry is about change, relationships, struggles, challenges and beyond. It is because I believe in quality of life that I care about those who communicate, listen, and work to reach people within our communities.

The ability to help others develop is a fundamental idea for any group or organization and it is a worthwhile effort despite difficulties. This allows time for reflection, study, research and helping others think differently. This model was not built without a lot of emotional and personal introspection. Throughout the process of writing this book, a mutual bonding took place and many new relationships were developed. Those persons that shared life stories, fears, and victories, where challenged to re-think what it means to connect with one another. This author reflecting on author ***Carlyle Fielding Stewart, III, in his book, Reclaiming What Was Lost, when he says:***

> ***INVESTMENT ALSO SUGGESTS A WILLINGNESS TO BE USED BY THE HOLY SPIRIT TO MAKE THE CHURCH BETTER THAN WE FOUND IT BY IMPROVING ITS QUALITY OF LIFE. TOO OFTEN, WE SIMPLY FIND OURSELVES MAINTAINING THE STATUS QUO. WHILE MAINTAINING A CHURCH IS BETTER THAN MAKING IT WORSE, A MORE BENEFICIAL APPROACH WOULD BE TO TRANSFORM THE CHURCH THROUGH A PERSONAL INVESTMENT OF TIME, INTELLECT, TALENT, AND RESOURCES.***

THIS AUTHOR IS REMINDED OF THOSE WORDS FROM 1 CORINTHIANS, CHAPTER 13:

> *"If I speak in the tongues of mortals and of angels, but do not have love, I am a noisy gong or a clanging cymbal. In addition;*

> *if I have prophetic powers and understand all mysteries and all knowledge, and if I have all faith, to remove mountains, but do not have love, I am nothing. If I give away all my possessions, and if I hand over my body so that I may boast, but do not have love, I gain nothing. Love is patient; love is kind; love is not envious or boastful or arrogant or rude. It does not insist on its own way; it is not irritable or resentful; it does not rejoice in wrongdoing, but believes all things, hopes all things, endures all things (1 Cor. 13:1-4).*

Future leaders in the church must begin to reflect upon the narratives of black theology, scripture, and creative opportunities for dialogue. Many people in our congregations need their voices to be heard and to be reflecting on the opportunities for making decisions in their congregations.

In the book, The Theology of the Cross for the 21st Century, by Alberto L. Garcia and A. R. Victor Raj, the authors assert:

> ***Black theology in United States begins with suffering and minor key moaning: the "torture tombs of slave ships," the experience of branded servitude, lynching, church-burning, non-suffrage, Jim Crow, second-class citizenship. Their way of speaking about God begins as a sung theology, feelings expressed by weeping exiles in psalms of deep lament, yearning for home, for Zion, for African.***

As this author reflects upon the question, ***"what does it means to be black and Christian in this global society?"*** he realizes that some folks may meet this unique challenge to be black and Christian. The late ***Dr. Samuel D. Proctor offered this compelling, compassionate, and comprehensive perspective:***

> ***WE FACE THE CHALLENGE OF BEING BOTH BLACK AND CHRISTIAN AT THE SAME TIME, BEARING OUR OWN BURDEN OF OPPRESSION WHILE HELPING OTHERS TO BE RELIEVED OF THEIRS; WE ARE FACED WITH DRYING OUR OWN TEARS OF FRUSTRATION AND FAILURE WHILE DRYING THE TEARS OF OTHERS; HERE WE ARE STRUGGLING TO OVERCOME OUR WON ESTRANGEMENT AND MARGINALITY WHILE TRYING TO CREATE A BLESSED COMMUNITY OUT OF (THE) POLARIZATION, TRIBALISM, AND XENOPHOBIA THAT SURROUND US. WE ARE INDEED THE WOUNDED HEALER. WE ARE THE VICTIMS OF WANTON HATRED WHILE CALLING OTHERS TO SELFLESS LOVE. WE ARE FALLING UNDER THE WEIGHT OF OUR OWN CROSSES WHILE BEING CALLED ON TO HELP SHOULDER THE CROSS OF SOMEONE ELSE. BLACK AND CHRISTIAN! WE ARE CALLED TO EACH OF OUR BROTHERS TO BE POSITIVE, CONSTRUCTIVE, AND NONVIOLENT, WHILE THEY ARE VICTIMS OF DENIAL, BENIGN NEGLECT, AND VIOLENCE.***

With respect to this book, this author is reminded of the term ***"life cycle of a congregation. "Robert Dale*** describes some concepts vital to these life cycles. He assures that the life cycle of a congregation is much like the steps and stages we might think of in our own human life cycle. The researcher uses examples of stages in human development by stating a parallel of the individual. He provides the following levels of growth: infant, toddler, and child, adolescent, young adult, adult, and older adult.

The author suggests that the congregations go through a period of life cycles and lists the following stages unique to this book for this author. The first stage is dream. ***Dream is the vision of what could be possible.*** The next stage is belief. ***Beliefs are the critical core values that keep the community alive and the ability to practice what the organization stands for.*** These are the concepts that will help the congregation live out the dream. These are the core-shared concepts that help people in community share their concerns and desires. This is a way to bring critical opportunities for change and new ideas. The next stage is goals and structure. ***This is the concept of helping the congregation have a vision for setting goals to bring about community.*** This is a stage of high energy where people are working in relationship to realize the dream. This is an important point of this life cycle as the fulfillment of a dream realized.

When the stages of ministry are reached, the goal is accomplished. The energy of hope is available, and people are ready for action.

The most important aspect of this life cycle is the power of ministry and provisioning and restructuring relationships. ***What is God asking of the people?*** In addition, ***what is the next step?*** Strong leadership helps folks realize that provisioning is moving with the word of God and making sure that nostalgia is an opportunity to move forward and make a difference. In other words, leaders and members need to risk moving beyond the concern of hope and seek ways for future leadership.

In a January 27, 2005, lecture entitled "Issues in 21st Century Leadership, Phase V Core Course, United Theological Seminary," Dr. G. Edwin Zeiders assures:

> ***Traditional congregations are defined as local churches that primarily express their life with a focus upon membership, money, and maintenance. These congregations repeat the same patterns repeatedly. They are predictable, usually stable, but often dying a slow death. Such congregations focus more upon the past and constantly remember the way things once were. Here the emphasis is***

> ***UPON VOLUNTEERING, MAINTAINING COMMITTEES AND REPEATING THE USUAL PROGRAMS YEAR AFTER YEAR WITH ESSENTIALLY THE SAME PEOPLE INVOLVED.***

The challenge for building relationships and group study and dialogue, change is always a difficult process. Changing the way people think and act is not easy. Relationships are hard when it comes to developing leaders for service. Relationships do not happen because of change and the leadership. Leaders and members need to do the hard work to continue the process of communication and think about their future. Leaders need to model positive relationships in the church setting.

Carlyle Fielding Stewart, III, in his book, Reclaiming What Was Lost: Recovering Spiritual Vitality in the Mainline Church, he assures in his chapter on reclaiming the importance of the black church:

> ***COLLABORATIVE MODELS OF MINISTRY DO WORK WELL IN BLACK CHURCHES. THIS IN NO WAY MEANS TO OBVIATE THE ROLE OF LAITY IN SHAPING THE DIRECTION AND DESTINY OF BLACK CONGREGATIONS. HEALTHY CHURCHES DEVELOP PARTNERSHIPS OR COVENANTS BETWEEN PASTORS AND LAITY.***

As this author concludes this section, ***Galatians 6:17 says, "from now on, let no one make trouble for me; for I carry the marks of Jesus branded on my body."***The local church has invested into hope, courage, and commitment, but ***relationships are the key to success.*** This requires working through conflict, new ideas, and challenges. Sometimes it hurts, and it requires courage in the face of the unknown. It will also require scars of hope and justice. ***James Alfred Smith, Sr., in the chapter entitled, "The Scars of Ministry," of his book, speak until Justice Wakes, assures:***

> ***Likewise, all who follow Jesus, including those who pastor God's people, will have scars on their souls to show that, like Jesus who called them, they have been wounded by many of the same people they have tried to assist, to bless, to coach, to direct, to encourage, to fertilize with the faith, to guide, to help, to inform and to inspire. Scars are visible symbols that some people are out to demoralize, defame, defeat, and destroy those who seek to utter a prophetic word.***

The late ***Dr. Samuel D. Proctor*** was the religious speaker for the 1996 commencement. ***Dr. Proctor*** spoke about how he encouraged many students toward higher education and the ability to rise above where we are and help someone along the way. After the day and ***Dr. Proctor*** was preparing to leave as we departed to Rochester airport after that commencement weekend. ***Dr. Proctor*** wrote these words in his book, ***"The Substance of Things Hoped for "friend" and "yoke-follower."*** As this writer reflects upon his role in ministry, it is more of being saddled together in a responsibility on continuing the unity that connected to building relationships. can generate energy that reached beyond one self and make a difference in the lives of others. It is important to have an intercultural communication perspective as one addresses the issues of change and growth. This book identified the needs for change through building relationships, producing new leaders, and improving working relationships.

Dr. William C. Turner, Jr., pastor of Mount Level Missionary Baptist Church and associate professor of the practice of homiletics at the Duke University Divinity School, asserts:

> ***Life is not meant to be lived in isolation or by individuals whose only goal is to do their own thing. If we rear our children that way, they will not be able to cope with the crises they shall surely face. Living as God intends is more than being surrounded by mother, father, and children. It is more than being in a circle of blood relations. It takes a community to rear children and to give them the spiritual resources for living productive lives that bring the glory of God.***

A special convent that is deeply rooted in relationships runs at the core of what the New Testament speaks of as Koinonia fellowship.

Because of the continuing strength of the African-American church, custom and religious tradition, slavery has had a major impact on segregation and yet, the African-American tradition remains strong. Although slavery was an evil injustice, the struggle of pain and forgiveness is and continues to be, a theme of the church. For this author, ***African-American literature can bind the demons of mistrust and release the forgiveness that is essential to the healing process.*** In the chapter entitled, ***"The Spirit of Liberation" in Down, Up, and Over, Dr. Dwight Hopkins asserts:***

> ***In this believing of those without access to resources to live their full humanity, we discover a faith to act on the covenantal promise of Yahweh. The doctrine of liberation for those who believe and act on this faith: faith in liberation from personal and collective demons and for the practice of freedom in a new God-centered self and life.***

The underlying assumption is that a lack of teamwork and organizational development has lost a little of its passions in many of our small to medium conservative congregations. The churches have longed to appreciate the development of its leaders and to understand completely and holistically each other as leaders and lay folks. The opportunities for more insight in this area of reflection and dialogue are vital to the congregation's leadership. This book provides the opportunity to review how congregations and churches that are traditional deal with postmodern issues surrounding the church for congregational development. This author's belief and premise is that a congregation is always developing, exploring, and learning how to meet the challenges in an urban intercultural communication society. This, then, led to a research-based approach of the themes and meaning for the traditional black church in our global society.

My reading of ***Dr. Carl Dudley. His book, Studying Congregations: A New Hand-Book was a good place to start. Dudley asserts,*** "Theology can be the springboard for spiritual renewal and revitalization of a congregation." The researcher's motivation came from the book, ***Saving Souls, Saving Society, by Dr. Heidi Unruh. He asserts:***

> ***CONGREGATES NEED TO SEEK NEW OPPORTUNITIES FOR LEARNING WITHOUT FOLLOWING OLD RULES. THIS ASSUMPTION HELPED TO EXPLORE WAYS OF ADDRESSING THE ISSUE OF CHANGE WITH THE ABILITY TO REFLECT, CONNECT AND DECIDE AND TO DO.***

There are four vital implications from this volume of Paradigm Shift. ***First***, the book is a valuable tool for assessing the issues of behavior, commitment, and responsiveness as it relates as to how people response to the issues impacting traditional congregation of it's people to continue service.

Second, the support of grassroots, non-profit agencies, and assistance church leaders to reflect on the importance of relationships and how effective Christian leaders work with others in the wider community.

Third, the local conservative churches have the ability to know that a conscious ability to relate on some common ground should reach for theological, biblical and evangelizing is vital to church growth. If the idea of church growth is rooted into the basic idea of simply, "this is our church, or we've never done it, that way, before" then little change is possible.

Fourth, the effort to continue moving the congregation toward connectedness and engaging the issues of the church and community.

BIBLIOGRAPHY

Agar, Michael H. *The Professional Stranger: An Informal Introduction to Ethnography,* 2d ed. Orlando, Florida: Academic Press, Inc., 1996.

Ammerman, Jackson, Jackson W. Carroll, Carl S. Dudley, and William McKinney. *Studying Congregations: A New Handbook: Nashville,* TN: Abingdon Press, 1998.

Billingsley, Andrew, *Mighty Like a River: The Black Church and Social Reform.* New York: Oxford University Press, 2000, accessed 24 October 2004 http: hirr.hartsem.edu/about/about_orw_con-re [prt.html; Internet.

Cannon, Katie G. *Black Womanish Ethics. American Academy of Religion Academy Series,* ed. Susan Thistle Thwaite, no. 60. Atlanta, GA: Scholars Press, 1988.

Cone, James. *God of the Oppressed.* New York: Orbis Books, 1975.

_________ *A Black Theology of Liberation (Maryknoll, NY: Orbis, 1986), 38.*

Conn, Harvie M., and Manuel Ortiz, *Urban Ministry* (Downers, IL: Intervarsity, 2001), 150.

Cox, Harvey. *"On the Future of Liberation Theologies."* Final reflection paper written for "Voices of Liberation," spring 1999 semester, Harvard Divinity School.

Dixie, Quinton Hosford, and Cornel West. *The Courage to Hope: From Black Suffering to Human Redemption.* Boston, MA: Beacon Press, 1999.

Douglas, Kelly Brown, and Ronald E. Hopson. *"Understanding the Black Church: The Dynamics of Change. "The Journal of Religious Thought* 8: 18-21.

Dudley, Carl. *From Typical Church to Social Ministry: A Study of the Elements Which Mobilize Congregations Review of Religious Research 2,* no. 3 (March 1991): 195.

Evans, James H., *We Have Been Believers* (Minneapolis, MN: Augsburg Fortress, 1992), 127.

Freire, Paulo. *Pedagogy of the Oppressed.* New York: Continuum, 2002.

Friedman, Edwin H. *Generation to Generation: Family Process in Church and Synagogue* New York: The Guilford Press, 1985.

Gilkes, Cheryl T. *If It Wasn't for The Women: Ministry Hearing and Empowering Black Poor Women.* Maryknoll, NY: Orbis, 2000.

Gustavo, Gutierrez. *The Power of the Poor in History.* Maryknoll, NY: Orbis Books, 1988.

Harris, Forrest E. *Ministry for Social Crisis.* Macon, GA: Mercer University Press, 1993.

Herzog, William, *Jesus, Justice, and the Reign of God* (Louisville, KY: John Knox, 2000), 168.

Hopkins, Dwight. *Down, Up, and Over: Slave Religion and Black Theology.* Minneapolis, MN: Fortress Press, 2000.

________. *Heart and Head.* New York: Palgrave, 2002.

Laruen, Cleophus. *The Heart and Black Preaching.* Louisville, KY: Westminster, 2000.

McKim, Donald K. *The Bible in Theology and Preaching.* Eugene, OR: Wipf and Stock Publishers, 1999.

Nunes, John. *The Theology of the Cross for the 21th Century, The African American and the Theology of the Cross,* eds. Alberto L. Garcia and A. R. Victor Raj. Saint Louis, MO: Concordia Press, 2002.

Ortiz, Manuel, and H. Conn, *Urban Ministry: The Kingdom, the City, and the People of God* (Downers Grove, IL: Intervarsity Press, 2001), 148.

Price, Elizabeth. "*Cognitive Complexity and the Learning Congregation.*" *An Interfaith Journal of Spirituality Growth and Transformation* 99, no. 4 (Fall 2004): 358.

Rauschenbusch, Walter. *A Theology for the Social Gospel.* Louisville, KY: Westminster John Knox, 1997.

Rundle, Gilbert R. *Leading Change in the Congregation: Spiritual and Organization Tools for Leaders.* Washington, DC: The Alban Institute, 2002.

Roberts, J. Deotis. *Black Theology in Dialogue.* Philadelphia, PA: Westminster, 1987.

Sanders, Cheryl, ed. *Living the Intersection: Womanish and Afro centrism in Theology.* Minneapolis, MN: Fortress Press, 1995.

Schein, Edgar H., *Organizational Culture, and Leadership* (San Francisco, CA: Jossey-Bass Publishers, 1992), 298-299.

Smith, Sr., James Alfred. *Speak Until Justice Wakes: Prophetic Reflections from J. Alfred Smith Sr.*, ed. Jini M. Kilgore. Valley Forge, PA: Judson Press, 2006.

Smith, Wallace Charles, *The Church in the Life of the Black Family* (Valley Forge, PA: Judson Press 1985) 23.

Stambaugh, John and David Balch, *The New Testament in Its Social Environment* (Philadelphia, PA: Westminster, 1986), 110.

Steward, Carlyle Fielding. *Reclaiming What Was Lost: Recovering Spiritual Vitality in the Mainline Church.* Nashville: Abingdon Press, 2003.

Stevens, R. Paul, and Phil Collins. *The Equipping Pastor.* Washington, DC: The Alban Institute, 1993.

The New National *Baptist Hymnal.* Nashville, TN: Triad Publication, 2001.

Thomas, Linda E., ed. *Living Stones in the Household of God: The Future of Black Theology.* Minneapolis, MN: Fortress Press, 2004.

Turner, William J., *Discipleship for African American Christians: Journal through the Church Covenant.* Valley Forge: Judson Press, 2002.

Unruh, Heidi Rolland, and Ronald J. *Sider. Saving Souls, Saving Society: Exploring the Spiritual and Social Dynamics of Church –Based Community Activism.* Proceedings at the Religious Research Association in Boston, Massachusetts, November 6, 1999, by Eastern Baptist Theological Seminary.

Walker, Alice. *In Search of Our Mother's Garden.* New York: Harcourt Brace and Jovanovich, 1983.

Wilmore, Giraud S. Black Religion, and Black Radicalism: *An Interpretation of the Religious History of Afro-American People,* 2nd ed. Maryknoll, NY: Orbis, 1983.

Zeiders, Dr. G. Edwin. *"Reshaping the Clay,"* Doctor of Ministry Intensive, United Theological Seminary, January 27, 2005. Lecture.

Author:

Johnny M. Wilson Jr Senior Pastor of Olney Street Baptist Church in Providence, Rhode Island. An ordained minister in American Baptist Churches, USA, he is the author of *Paradigm Shift: Building A Foundation of Church Leadership from the Inside Out.* He received an M.Div. from American Baptist Seminary of the West, Berkeley, California and a Doctor of Ministry from United Theological Seminary, Dayton, OH. Dr. Wilson is an 2015 fellow of Princeton Theological Seminary, Princeton, New Jersey.

www.ingramcontent.com/pod-product-compliance
Lightning Source LLC
Chambersburg PA
CBHW020333130626
46549CB00003B/1154
9786214340521